I0786569

Wealthy Lotus

You're amazing
just the
way you
are.

www.ingramcontent.com/pod-product-compliance
Lightning Source LLC
Chambersburg PA
CBHW080027260726
48658CB00007B/2501
9781723967467